From Octop...

Squid Cookbook

Simple, Inventive Delicious Octopus Recipes
That Will Leave Your Guests Wanting More

BY

Stephanie Sharp

License Notes

wwwwwwwwwwwwwwwwwwwwwwwwwwwwwwwww

Table of Contents

Introduction

Far too many persons live in a state of ill health, moderate obesity and lethargy. Many live with back pains, grave headaches, arthritis, high blood pressure, inflammation, skin problems, diabetes, high cholesterol, cancer and insomnia – all are the byproducts of the new type of western diet, processed food. The recipes in Octopus Cookbook can assist you with these symptoms.

Octopus Cookbook contains over 30 recipes created with you in mind. The meals are simple, easy to prepare, delicious and healthy. The recipes are geared to bring an astonishing amount of minerals, essential fatty acids (omega 3), antioxidants, vitamins and more.

Calamari Marinara

There are multiple ways to cook Calamari. Here is a simple recipe for you to try.

Serves: 4

Time: 1 hr. 11 mins

Ingredients

- 2 tbsps. olive oil
- 1 onion, yellow, thinly sliced
- 1 chile pepper, serrano, thinly sliced
- 3 garlic cloves, minced
- 1 anchovy fillet
- 1/2 tsp. red pepper flakes
- 1/2 tsp. kosher salt, plus more as needed
- 1/2 cup dry white wine
- 1 cup clam juice
- 6 cups Italian plum tomatoes, pureed
- 1/2 tsp. oregano, dried
- 2 lbs. frozen calamari, thawed and sliced into thick pieces
- 1/4 cup Italian parsley, chopped
- Parmigiano-Reggiano cheese, grated (optional)
- 1 (16 oz.) package dry pasta

Directions

1. In a saucepan off heat, drizzle olive oil. Add salt, red pepper flakes, anchovy fillet, garlic, serrano pepper, and onions.

2. Put pot on medium-high heat. After a minute or so when onions begin to sizzle, sauté onions for 3-4 minutes until garlic and onions begin to turn golden. Mix in wine.

3. Cook for 3-5 minutes until wine reduces to half. Add then simmer oregano, tomatoes, and clam juice on medium-high heat. As sauce starts to bubble, bring heat to medium-low. Gently simmer for about 15 minutes.

4. Put calamari in a sauce pot, gently stirring. Simmer for 35-45 minutes until calamari becomes tender. Take off heat. Mix in parsley.

5. Boil a big pot of lightly salted water. Cook spaghetti in boiling water, occasionally stirring, for about 12 minutes until firm to chew and tender. Drain.

6. Stir some sauce in hot and drained pasta. Put in warm bowls. Top with grated cheese and more marinara sauce.

Grilled Calamari with White Beans

For a new and innovative dinner option try this Calamari and Beans recipe.

Serves: 6

Time: 3 hrs. 30 mins

Ingredients

- 1 cup white beans, dried
- 1 onion, medium, quartered
- 3 thyme sprigs
- 1 bay leaf
- 7 tbsps. olive oil, extra-virgin
- 2 large shallots, chopped
- 1 lb. calamari, cleaned
- 1/2 cup fresh lemon juice
- 2 garlic cloves, minced
- 1/4 cup Italian parsley, chopped
- 1/4 tsp. red pepper, dried, crushed

Directions

1. In a big saucepan, add beans. Cover beans in water to cover about 3 inches. Boil. Take off heat. Cover and stand for 1 hour.

2. Add bay leaf, thyme, and onion. Simmer for about 1 hour and 15 minutes, occasionally stirring, until beans are soft. Drain.

3. Throw out bay leaf, thyme, and onion. Place beans in saucepan.

4. In a small skillet, heat 2 tbsps. oil on medium heat. Add shallots. Sauté for about 4 minutes until tender.

5. Mix shallots into beans. Season with pepper and salt. You can make this 1 day in advanced, covered and chilled. Re-warm on medium-low heat, mixing and adding extra water if needed prior to serving.

6. In a medium bowl, put calamari tentacles. Slice calamari bodies in half, lengthwise. Put in bowl. Add 2 tbsps. oil, garlic, and lemon juice. Toss until coated. Stand for 1 hour.

7. Heat barbecue to medium-high heat. Drain calamari then sprinkle pepper and salt. Grill for about 30 seconds per side until edges slightly curled.

8. Mix parsley in warm beans. Distribute beans to 6 plates. Top using calamari. Drizzle 3 tbsp. oil on. Sprinkle crushed red pepper.

Angel-hair Pasta with Sautéed Octopus

You can use fresh octopus to make this pasta extra special.

Serves: 8

Time: 1 hr. 30 mins

Ingredients

- 1/2 small onion, chopped
- 3 garlic cloves, chopped
- 1 tbsp. olive oil
- 1 1/2 lb. tomatoes, chopped coarsely
- 1/2 tsp. fine sea salt
- 1 1/2 lb. cleaned large octopus, rinsed well
- 1/2 tsp. fine sea salt
- 1/4 cup extra-virgin olive oil
- 1/2 small onion, finely chopped
- 1/4 cup parsley, chopped finely, flat-leaf
- 1 small leek (green part only), cleaned and chopped finely
- 1 garlic clove, finely chopped
- 1 tbsp. olive oil
- 1/2 lb. flounder bones and trimmings
- 3 cups water
- 1 cup dry white wine
- 1/2 tsp. fine sea salt
- 1 medium onion, minced
- 2 garlic cloves, minced
- 2 tbsps. extra-virgin olive oil
- 1/2 tsp. fine sea salt, or to taste

- 8 oz capellini, broken into 2-inch pieces

Directions

To make tomato sauce:

1. Sauté garlic and onion in a 3-quart heavy saucepan in oil on -moderately low heat stirring for about 3 minutes until soft.

2. Add tomatoes, with water if canned, and the sea salt. Simmer, occasionally stirring to break tomatoes up, covered, for 40 minutes.

3. In a blender, puree sauce, being careful if it's hot. Run through a fine sieve then discard remaining solids.

Octopus:

4. Chop octopus tentacles finely. Chill until ready to use later for pasta or fish stock. Cut open octopus bodies using kitchen shears. Rinse insides well then pat dry bodies.

5. Lay flat each body flat on a cutting board, interior side up, cutting lengthwise including flap, to thin strips like spaghetti (less than 1/8-inch wide) using a sharp knife.

6. Chill strips while covered until you're ready to use them.

Stock:

7. Cook garlic, leek greens, and onion in a 3-4-quart heavy saucepan in oil on moderately low heat for about 3 minutes until soft.

8. Add fish trimmings and bones and half of chopped tentacles. Cook, occasionally stirring, for about 2 minutes, covered, until tentacles release its liquid.

9. Add sea salt, wine, and water. Simmer, skimming the froth.

10. Take off from heat and stand for 15 minutes, uncovered. Pour stock into a bowl through a fine sieve. Press on and get rid of solids.

Pasta:

11. Sauté garlic and onion in a deep 12-inch heavy skillet in oil on moderate heat for 3-5 minutes until very soft. Add leftover chopped tentacles.

12. Cook, while stirring, until liquid has been released (about 2 minutes). Add sea salt, 3 cups fish stock, and 1 1/2 cups tomato sauce boil and stir occasionally. Mix in pasta and boil, stirring. Take off from heat and stand for about 5 minutes, covered, until pasta gets cooked through.

13. Sauté octopus as pasta stands. With sea salt toss octopus strips. Set your oil on to heat up in a nonstick skillet on high heat until hot yet not smoking.

14. Sauté garlic for about 1 minute, stirring until golden. Add parsley and octopus, sauté for 30 seconds.

15. Octopus will continue to cook from the residual heat and will still be partly translucent.

16. Place octopus on top of pasta and immediately serve.

Holiday Calamari Salad

This salad is perfect to enjoy over the holidays.

Serves: 12

Time: 25m

Ingredients

- 2 lemons, juiced
- 6 garlic cloves, peeled, minced
- 1 sprig parsley, chopped
- pepper to taste
- salt to taste
- 3 lbs. squid, cleaned and sliced
- 2.25 oz. black olives, canned, pitted
- 4 stalks celery, chopped

Directions

1. Mix parsley, garlic, and lemon juice in a medium bowl. Season with pepper and salt.

2. Boil a medium pot of water. Mix in squid. Cook until tender for about 3 minutes. Drain.

3. Toss lemon juice mixture, celery, olives, and squid. Cover and keep in fridge to chill. Serve.

Authentic Seafood Paella

Paella is a classic dish in Spanish cuisine that is perfect for dinner guests.

Serves: 2

Time: 55 mins

Ingredients

- 2 tbsps. olive oil
- 1 onion, finely diced
- 1/2 tomato, finely diced
- 1 pinch salt
- 1/2 tbsp. smoked paprika
- 6 fresh Romano
- 1/2 cup butter beans, canned, drained and rinsed
- 1/2 cup white rice
- 6 large shrimp
- 6 mussels
- 6 clams
- 1 cup white wine
- 2 cups seafood stock
- 1 pinch Saffron thread
- 1 tsp. rosemary, chopped finely
- 1 cup peas
- 5 baby squid tentacles, cut into rings
- 8 lemon wedges
- 1 tbsp. chopped fresh flat-leaf parsley

Directions

1. In a big skillet or paella pan, heat olive oil on high heat. Sauté smoked paprika, tomato, salt, and onion in hot oil for about 3 minutes until soft.

2. Add rice, butter beans, and Romano beans. Stir and cook for 2-3 minutes until rice gets coated in oil.

3. Put clams, mussels, and shrimp on top of rice mixture. Pour seafood stock and white wine in. Sprinkle rosemary and saffron threads. Simmer mixture. Flip shellfish.

4. Keep cooking for about 5 minutes until mussels and clams opened and shrimp are cooked and pink. Take out shrimp, mussels, and clams. Put aside.

5. Mix peas into paella. Simmer for 20-25 minutes, uncovered, until rice absorbs liquid and is tender. Mix in squid.

6. Put shrimp, mussels, and clams back in the pan. Cook for 2-3 more minutes until squid is cooked through and opaque.

7. Serve with chopped parsley and lemon wedges.

Grilled Calamari Arugula Salad

Healthy, quick to prepare and delicious.

Serves: 4

Time: 40 mins

Ingredients

- 1 1/2 lbs. squid, cleaned
- 1/2 lb. arugula
- 3 lemons
- 1 garlic clove, large, minced
- 1/2 cup olive oil, extra-virgin

Directions

1. Prep your grill to cook. Open bottom vents of grill if you're using a charcoal grill.

2. Rinse squid in cold running water. Pat dry using paper towels. For big squids, halve tentacles, lengthwise, then slice longer ones if they're still attached to 2-inch pieces, crosswise.

3. Squeeze 2 lemons to get 1/4 cup of juice. Cut leftover whole lemons to wedges.

4. Whisk 1/8 tsp. pepper, 1/2 tsp. salt, garlic, oil, and lemon juice until well combined. Place 1/4 cup dressing in a big shallow bowl, keeping the rest. In a shallow bowl, toss squid to the dressing until coated. Marinate in room temperature for 10 minutes, flipping once.

5. Through every squids' body, thread 2 skewers, near the opposite site of the body to keep squid flat as you grill. Thread all flaps to 1or 2 skewers. Thread all the tentacles on skewers, crosswise through the thickest part, letting tentacles dangle, without crowding. Throw out marinade.

6. When fire's hot (a hand can be held 5 inches on top of the rack for 1-2 seconds only), grill squid on grill rack that's lightly oiled. Cook for 1-1 1/2 minutes in total, flipping once, uncovered, until they turned opaque. Place on a cutting board and take out skewers. Cut squid bodies to 1 1/2-inch-thick strips, lengthwise. Cut strips in half crosswise if the squid is big.

7. In a clean bowl, toss pepper, salt, 3 tbsps. reserved dressing and squid. In another bowl, toss arugula with enough or left over dressing until coated. Season with pepper and salt.

8. Distribute arugula to 4 plates. Top using squid. Serve alongside lemon wedges.

Calamari in Red Wine and Tomato Sauce

Use your favorite tomato or spaghetti sauce for the base.

Serves: 6

Time: 45 mins

Ingredients

- 2 lbs. calamari, cleaned
- 4 cups tomato sauce
- 1 cup Chianti wine
- 2 tbsps. fresh lemon juice
- 1 tbsp. olive oil
- 2 tsps. chopped garlic
- 1 tsp. ground black pepper
- 1/2 tsp. ground cayenne pepper
- 1 tsp. dried basil
- 1/3 cup grated Romano cheese

Direction

1. Separate tentacles from long body of calamari if not yet done. Slice body or tubes to rings, 1/2-2/3-inch thick. Put aside.

2. Mix cheese, basil, cayenne pepper, black pepper, garlic, olive oil, lemon juice, red wine, and tomato sauce in a saucepan.

3. Simmer for about 30 minutes on medium low to evaporate the wines' alcohol and blend all the flavors.

4. Add calamari to sauce. Keep on to slowly simmer for about another 20-30 minutes, occasionally stirring.

NB: It's done when calamari are opaque and plump. Don't cook on higher heat or for longer time because calamari are well-known for becoming rubbery.

Banana Leaf Seafood

This Banana Leaf Seafood is great for diners of all ages.

Serves: 2

Time: 4 hrs. 30 mins

Ingredients

- 6 shallots, finely chopped
- 4 cloves garlic, peeled and crushed
- 2 tbsps. sambal belachan
- 2 tsps. vegetable oil
- 1 tsp. curry powder
- 1 tsp. ground cumin
- 1 tsp. lime juice
- Pepper, to taste
- salt, to taste
- 1 lb. squid, cleaned and sliced into rings
- 1 banana leaf

Directions

1. Mix shallots, pepper, salt, lime juice, cumin, curry powder, vegetable oil, sambal belachan, and garlic in a medium, non-reactive bowl.

2. Put squid in mixture. Cover.

3. Marinate for at least 2 hours.

4. Preheat an outdoor grill to high heat. Oil grate lightly.

5. Grease banana leaf lightly. Wrap leaf around squid. Place on the grill. Cook for 10-15 minutes until squid is opaque and leaf is charred slightly.

Curried Squid in Betel Leaf Wraps

This appetizer comprises a mix of spicy squid and cooling relish wrapped up in betel leaves.

Serves: 8

Time: 10 mins

Ingredients

- 2 tbsps. white vinegar, distilled
- 2 tbsps. sugar
- 1/2 cup Persian cucumber, unpeeled, diced finely
- 1/2 cup celery, diced finely
- 10 long cilantro stems, chopped
- 2 garlic cloves, halved
- 2 1-inched pieces ginger, peeled, chopped
- 2 tbsps. vegetable oil
- 1 tbsp. Curry Powder
- 8 oz. squid bodies, cleaned, cut into thick rings
- 2 jalapeño chiles, red, seeded, cut into strips
- 1 tbsp. fish sauce
- 1 tbsp. oyster sauce
- 1 tsp. sugar
- 1/2 cup coconut cream
- 2 tbsps. chicken broth, low-salt
- 16 betel leaves

Directions

Relish:

1. Stir sugar and vinegar together in a little bowl until the sugar has dissolved then set it aside to be used as dressing.

2. In a different small bowl, mix ginger, celery, chile and cucumber together then mix the dressing in by the spoonful, stopping when taste is as desired.

Wraps:

3. Mix ginger, garlic and cilantro stems together in the mini processor and grind until it turns into a paste.

4. In a big, sturdy skillet over medium-high heat, heat the oil and stir the cilantro paste in for 1 minute. Stir the curry powder in for 30 seconds.

5. Mix chile strips and squid in and stir-fry for 1 minute or until squid is nearly tender. Stir in sugar, oyster sauce, coconut cream, fish sauce and chicken broth for 1 minute until the sauce thickens a little.

6. Place the betel leaves on a platter and put the squid mixture on top of each leaf using a slotted spoon. Set the relish over it with a spoon.

Buttermilk-Battered Calamari

Simple battered calamari make the best snack when served with marina sauce.

Serves: 6

Time: 15 mins

Ingredients

- 1 cup buttermilk
- 1 cup flour, all-purpose
- 1/2 tbsp. salt
- 1/2 tbsp. black pepper, ground
- 1 tsp. oregano, dried
- 1 lb. octopus, cleaned, cut into thick rings
- 2 cups vegetable oil for frying

Directions

1. In a deep-fryer or saucepan, heat oil to 190 degrees C/375 degrees F.

2. Put buttermilk in a medium bowl. Mix oregano, pepper, salt, and flour in another bowl. Submerge octopus rings in buttermilk, then coat in seasoned flour.

3. Place coated pieces in hot oil. In small batches, fry and turning if needed to evenly cook. Drain on paper towels when browned evenly.

4. Repeat process with leftover octopus. Serve while hot.

Fried Squid and Aioli

Super crispy squid with a delicious aioli dip.

Serves: 4

Time: 20 mins

Ingredients

- 1 1/4 tsps. baking powder
- 1 3/4 cups flour, arepa, divided
- 1 egg yolk, large
- 2/3 cup potato starch
- 1/4 cup olive oil
- 1 garlic clove, grated finely
- 1 tsp. lemon juice
- 1/2 cup grapeseed oil
- Kosher salt
- Vegetable oil (for frying; about 8 cups)
- 6 oz. squid, bodies and tentacles separated
- 4 scallions, sliced into 3-inch pieces
- 4 very lemon wheels, thin
- 1/3 cup basil leaves, torn

Directions

1. Mix 3/4 cup of arepa flour, baking powder, and potato starch in a big bowl. Mix in 2 1/3 cups of water. Allow to sit for 30 minutes so the flour hydrates. Put leftover cup of arepa flour into a shallow bowl.

2. While that happens, mix lemon juice, garlic, and egg yolk in a small bowl until combined. Constantly whisking, slowly drizzle olive oil and grapeseed oil. Mix until sauce becomes emulsified and thick. Season the aioli with salt then mix in a tsp. of water.

3. Put a thermometer on a big pot. Put in 3 inches of vegetable oil. Heat on medium-high until the thermometer says 375 degrees F.

4. While it heats, cut the squid. Slice the bodies lengthwise on one side then open to reveal the inside. Cut in half crosswise, or into thirds if it's big. Cut every half or third to triangles that are 1 1/2 inches. Cut the tentacles in half. Rinse then pat dry.

5. Cook in batches of 5-6 and bring the oil back to 375 degrees F between the batches. Submerge the lemon, scallions, and squid in the arepa flour and shake off the excess. Dip in the batter, allow excess to drip off. Fry for around 2 minutes, turning in every 30 second or so, until puffed, crisp, and golden.

6. Place on paper towels. Season using salt. Top using basil and serve with aioli.

Buttermilk Calamari Green Salad

Enjoy a crispy crunch by adding buttermilk calamari with your green salad.

Serves: 4

Time: 15 mins

Ingredients

- 2 cups buttermilk
- 2 cups flour, all-purpose
- 4 cups vegetable oil (for frying)
- 1 lb. octopus, bodies, cleaned, cut into thick rings (keep tentacles intact)
- 5 oz. baby greens, mixed
- Leek Dressing
- 2 plum tomatoes, seeded, chopped

Directions

1. Place buttermilk in a big bowl. Put flour in a separate big bowl. Season flour using pepper and salt. In a heavy big saucepan, pour vegetable oil.

2. Heat to 375 degrees F. In batches, dip calamari pieces in buttermilk, coat by turning. Take out then coat in flour, shaking excess off.

3. Add calamari carefully in the saucepan. Fry for about 1 minute until golden brown.

4. Use a slotted spoon to place on paper towels; drain. Repeat process with leftover flour, buttermilk, and calamari.

5. Distribute greens on 4 plates. Put calamari equally on greens. Place leek dressing on salad using spoon. Garnish with chopped tomatoes and serve.

Fried Calamari Salad

For a healthier lunch, try this Fried Calamari Salad.

Serves: 8

Time: 20 mins

Ingredients

- 1/4 cup orange juice concentrate
- 2 tbsps. light miso, yellow
- 1 tbsp. ginger, peeled, minced
- 1/2 cup rice vinegar
- 2 tsps. sugar
- 2 garlic cloves, minced
- 1 tsp. hot chili oil*
- 1/2 cup vegetable oil
- 1 chayote squash, peeled, cored, diced
- 1 head curly endive, sliced thinly
- 1 head radicchio, sliced thinly
- 1 1/3 cups canned hearts of palm, drained, sliced
- 1/3 cup mint, chopped
- 1/2 cup flour, all purpose
- 1/2 cup cornstarch
- Vegetable oil (for frying)
- 2 lbs. calamari, cleaned, cut into rings
- 1/2 cup flaked sweetened coconut
- 1 cup cashews, roasted, lightly salted

Directions

1. Dressing: mix initial 7 ingredients in a medium-sized bowl until miso is melted. Slowly mix in half a cup of vegetable oil.

2. Salad: cook chayote in a medium saucepan full of boiling salted water for around 5 minutes until tender. Drain and cool. Combine mint, hearts of palm, radicchio, endive, and chayote in a big bowl.

3. Mix cornstarch and flour in a pie dish. Add 3 inches of oil in a heavy big pot. Sprinkle the calamari with pepper and salt. Coat calamari in flour mixture. Shake excess off. In batches, put calamari in the pot and deep-fry for around 3 minutes for every batch until brown and crisp. Use a slotted spoon to move calamari on paper towels to drain.

4. Put calamari in a bowl with the chayote salad. Add 2/3 cup of dressing, cashews, calamari then coat by tossing. Divide salad to 8 plates then serve.

Calamari

A delicious yet simple recipe.

Serves: 10

Time: 20 mins

Ingredients

- 12 squid, cleaned, cut into rings
- 1/2 tsp. black pepper, ground
- 3 cups vegetable oil
- 1/4 cup flour, all-purpose
- 1 tsp. oregano, dried
- 1 tsp. salt
- 8 lemon wedges, for garnish

Directions

1. In a pot or heavy, deep frying pan, preheat oil. It should be 365 degrees F.

2. Mix black pepper, oregano, salt, and flour in a medium-sized mixing bowl. Coat squid with spice and flour mixture.

3. Cook squid in oil until light brown for 2-3 minutes. Avoid overcooking for the squid not to be though. Dry on paper towels.

4. Serve with lemon wedges.

Deep-fried Calamari Rings

Tasty yet easy deep fried calamari rings.

Serves: 4

Time: 20 mins

Ingredients

- 1 cup all-purpose flour
- 2 tsps. salt
- 1 tsp. paprika
- 1/4 tsp. ground black pepper
- 1 tsp. garlic powder
- 6 cups vegetable oil for frying
- 12 oz. calamari rings
- salt to taste
- 2 tbsps. cocktail sauce, or to taste
- 1 quartered lemon

Directions

1. In a shallow bowl. Stir black pepper, paprika, 2 tsps. salt, and flour together.

2. In a big saucepan or deep-fryer, heat oil to 190 degrees C/375 degrees F.

3. Evenly coat calamari rings in flour mixture, shake off excess flour.

4. In batches, fry calamari rings for 3-4 minutes in hot oil until golden brown. Place cooked calamari on a plate lined with paper towels. Sprinkle salt.

5. Serve calamari with lemon wedges and a cocktail.

Calamari in A Creamy White Wine Sauce

This Calamari recipe is easy to whip up and is super delicious.

Serves: 2

Time: 35 mins

Ingredients

- 1/2 lb. linguine pasta
- 2 tbsps. olive oil
- 3 garlic cloves, crushed
- 8 oz. squid, cleaned, body cut in thick rings, tentacles whole
- 3/4 cup white wine
- 3 cherry peppers, sliced thinly
- 2 tbsps. cornstarch
- 1 cup cream
- red pepper flakes, crushed, to taste
- pepper, to taste
- salt, to taste
- 1/2 cup basil, shredded
- 1/4 cup Parmesan cheese, grated

Directions

1. Place lightly salted water in a large pot and make it boil. Place pasta and cook for 8-10 minutes or until al dente; strain.

2. Set your olive oil on medium heat in a skillet to get hot.

3. Put in crushed garlic and cook for a couple of seconds until it becomes golden brown in color.

4. Mix in the squid and cook until it becomes white. Stir in cherry pepper slices and white wine; gently boil and cook for 3 minutes until the wine is lessened by half.

5. Mix cornstarch into cream and mix it into the boiling calamari. Use pepper, salt, basil and red pepper flakes to season; mix until thick. Toss pasta with sauce to serve and drizzle with Parmesan cheese.

Hassle Free Calamari

This recipe takes very little effort to produce an amazing dish.

Serves: 4

Time: 50 mins

Ingredients

- 1 cup ricotta cheese
- 1/3 cup mascarpone cheese
- 12 sun-dried tomatoes, chopped
- 1/2 cup dry breadcrumbs
- 1/4 tsp. dried oregano, or to taste
- 1 pinch salt and pepper to taste
- 8 large squid, cleaned and tentacles removed
- 2 tbsps. butter
- 2 cloves garlic, chopped
- 2 tbsps. sesame seeds

Directions

1. Preheat oven to 175 degrees C/350 degrees F. Mix pepper, salt, oregano, breadcrumbs, sun-dried tomatoes, mascarpone cheese, and ricotta cheese in a medium bowl until blended well. Put aside.

2. Boil a big pot of lightly salted water. Trim ends of squid bodies to make them evenly sized. Rinse tubes out.

3. Spoon cheese mixture in cavities of squid until full. Secure open ends using toothpicks. Put in a boiling water, cooking for 6 minutes.

4. Take out stuffed calamari tubes from water. Put on a baking dish. Bake in the preheated oven for 20 minutes.

5. In a big skillet, melt butter on medium heat. Add sesame seeds and garlic, put calamari tubes in the skillet, frying on all sides until they're golden brown. Take out toothpicks prior to serving.

Calamari Macaronatha

Here is an easy version of Calamari Macaronatha.

Serves: 4

Time: 55 mins

Ingredients

- 2 1/2 cups elbow macaroni
- 1 lb. octopus, cleaned
- 1/4 cup red wine vinegar
- 6 tbsps. extra virgin olive oil
- 4 cloves garlic, minced
- 1 large onion, chopped
- 1 1/2 cups crushed tomatoes
- 1/4 cup dry white wine
- 1/2 lemon, juiced
- 1 cinnamon stick, broken in half
- 2 bay leaves
- 1/4 tsp. dried basil leaves
- 1/2 tsp. oregano, dried
- Salt, to taste
- 1/2 cup grated Mizithra cheese
- Black Pepper, to taste

Directions

1. Set lightly salted water in a pot to boil. Add pasta then cook until al dente or for about 8-10 minutes. Drain.

2. Boil octopus in 3 cups of water mixed with red wine vinegar in a small saucepan for 8-10 minutes. Drain. Slice to bite-sized rings/pieces. Put aside.

3. In a big heavy skillet, heat olive oil. Sauté garlic and onion until onion is soft yet not brown. Mix in octopus.

4. Sauté for 2 minutes. Pour in lemon juice, white wine, and crushed tomatoes. Season with pepper, salt, oregano, basil, bay leaves, and cinnamon stick.

5. Once boiling, switch the heat to low then simmer for 15-20 minutes, occasionally stirring, partially covered.

6. Take off from heat. Mix in cooked pasta. Serve with grated cheese on top.

Amalfi Calamari Pasta

If you like calamari, then this recipe is perfect for you.

Serves: 6

Time: 45 mins

Ingredients

- 1 1/4 cups all-purpose flour
- 2 cups canola oil
- 1/4 cup cornstarch
- 1/2 cup Italian parsley, chopped, divided
- 1 tsp. coarse kosher salt
- 3 to 4 tbsps. fresh lemon juice
- 1/4 cup butter, unsalted, diced
- 1/2 tsp. baking powder
- 1/4 tsp. cayenne pepper
- 1 lb. squid (bodies only), cleaned. cut into thin rings
- 2 cups olive oil
- 1 lb. spaghetti
- Lemon wedges
- Deep-fry thermometer

Directions

1. Line multiple layers of paper towels on a rimmed baking sheet. Mix cayenne pepper, baking powder, a tsp. of coarse salt, cornstarch, and flour in a medium sized bowl.

2. Work in batches to toss the squid rings to coat in the flour mixture, then place the rings in one layer on a sheet of foil.

3. Pour both oils in a big skillet. Lean a deep-fry thermometer on a skillet's side, keeping the bulb in the oil.

4. Heat oil on medium-high heat until the thermometer hits 350-350 degrees F. Frying in multiple batches, add the squid rings in the hot oil and cook for 2-3 minutes for each batch until they're crisp around the edges and light golden.

5. Use a slotted spoon to move the squid to a baking sheet lined with paper towels to drain.

6. As it drains, cook the pasta in a big pot filled with boiling salted water. Occasionally stir until tender yet firm to chew. Drain, keeping a cup of pasta water. Place pasta back in the pot. Add 3 tbsps. of lemon juice and butter and coat pasta by tossing. Add 3/4 of pasta water and toss. Mix in 1/3 cup of parsley.

7. Adjust seasoning with pepper and coarse salt. Add extra lemon juice and pasta water if you want.

8. Place pasta in a big bowl. Top with calamari. Top with leftover parsley. Serve lemon wedges on the side.

Octopus Salad

Delicious octopus salad.

Serves: 8

Time: 25 mins

Ingredients

- 1/2 cup olive oil
- 1/4 cup red wine vinegar
- 2 garlic cloves, pressed
- 1 cup white wine, dry
- 1 cup water
- 1 lb. octopus, cleaned and cut into rings
- 1 cup celery, chopped
- 1/2 bunch cilantro, chopped
- 1 bell pepper, red, chopped
- 1 bell pepper, green, chopped
- 1 bell pepper, yellow, chopped
- 1 cup cucumber, chopped
- 1 bunch green onions, chopped
- 1 bunch parsley, chopped
- 1 cup jicama, peeled, shredded
- 1 jalapeno pepper, chopped finely

Directions

1. Mix garlic, red wine vinegar, and olive oil in a small bowl.

2. Put wine and water on a low boil in a medium saucepan. Mix in the octopus and cook for about 2 minutes until opaque. Drain then cool.

3. In a big bowl. Stir jalapeno, jicama, parsley, green onions, cucumber, cilantro, celery, and yellow, red, and green bell pepper.

4. Gently toss with octopus and olive oil dressing mixture. Chill prior to serving.

Caribbean Stewed Octopus

This octopus stew is mildly spicy yet sweet and will take you on an interesting food journey.

Serves: 4

Time: 3 hrs.

Ingredients

- 1/4 cup butter, divided
- 1 tbsp. olive oil
- 1 small onion, yellow, diced
- 1 lb. octopus, or more to taste
- 1 tsp. sea salt
- 1 cup crushed ice
- 2 tbsps. minced fresh ginger root
- 2 large cloves garlic, minced
- 750 ml white wine, dry

Directions

1. In a skillet, heat 1 tbsp. butter and oil on medium heat. Sauté onion in the oil and butter for about 5 minutes until soft and translucent.

2. Reduce heat down to low. Keep cooking, frequently stirring, for about 30 minutes more until onion is dark brown and very tender.

3. Rinse octopus. Put on a flat work surface. Slice tentacles to thirds. Chop head to bite-sized pieces.

4. Put octopus pieces in a resalable plastic bag that's gallon-sized. Mix salt in then add crushed ice. Seal bag and put in a bigger grocery bag.

5. Pound octopus with a meat mallet's smooth side until very tender. Take octopus out of bag and drain inside a colander.

6. Mix garlic and ginger into skillet with onion. Cook for 1-2 minutes until fragrant. Put in leftover 3 tbsps. butter and wine. Increase heat and boil. Add octopus.

7. Reduce heat to simmer. Cook, covered, mixing every 10 minutes for about 1 hour until flavors merge.

8. Uncover and keep simmering for about 1 hour more until sauce is thickened to your preference and octopus becomes tender.

Seafood Salad

This delicious salad is best served chilled and is super delicious.

Serves: 12

Time: 30 mins

Ingredients

- 1 lb. octopus, cleaned
- 1 lb. scallops, small, sea
- 1 lb. shrimp, medium, shelled
- 3/4 cup olive oil, extra-virgin
- 3/4 cup parsley, cleaned, chopped coarsely
- 1/2 cup chives, cleaned, chopped
- 1 tbsp. rosemary leaves, chopped
- 1/2 tsp. table salt
- 2 lemons, sliced thin
- fresh lemon juice to taste
- coarse sea salt to taste

Directions

1. Take flaps from octopus sacs if they're attached and put aside. Cut sacs into 1/4-inch thick rings, crosswise. Cut leftover flaps to strips that are 1/4-inch thick. Cut tentacles in half lengthwise if big. Take out tough muscle from side of every scallop if needed.

2. Prepare a big bowl of cold water and ice. Cook shrimp for 1 minute in a big saucepan with boiling salted water. Cook until pink and just cooked through. Place in ice water using a slotted spoon to halt cooking.

3. Put scallops in boiling water. Cook for 2 minutes at a bare simmer or until cooked through. Place scallops in ice water using a slotted spoon to halt cooking.

4. Add octopus to boiling water. Cook for 20-30 seconds or until just opaque. In a colander, drain octopus. Place in ice water to halt cooking.

5. In the colander, drain seafood well. Place in a bowl. Chill seafood until cold, covered for at least 2 hours, up to 1 day.

6. Herbed oil: Blend herbed oil ingredients in a blender on high speed for 1 minute. Pour oil through a fine sieve to a bowl, pressing hard on solids. Throw out solids.

7. You can make herbed oil 2 days in advanced, chilled and covered. One hour prior to serving, toss seafood with lemon slices and lemon juice. Distribute seafood to 12 bowls.

8. Drizzle herbed oil. Sprinkle salads using sea salt. Serve extra sea salt on the side.

Braised Squid

Simple and garlicky and succulent.

Serves: 6

Time: 15 mins

Ingredients

- 1 1/2 lbs. squid, cleaned
- 1/4 tsp. red-pepper flakes
- 2 cups parsley sprigs, flat-leaf, divided
- 5 garlic cloves
- 28-oz. whole tomatoes, canned, in juice, chopped coarsely
- 3 tbsps. olive oil
- 3/4 cup Chardonnay
- 1/4 cup water
- Accompaniment: crusty bread

Directions

1. Rinse squid in cold water. Pat dry. Cut big tentacles to half, lengthwise. Cut bodies and flaps, if they're there, to 1/2-inch- wide rings, crosswise.

2. Chop parsley to get 2 tbsp. Put aside. Chop leftover garlic and parsley together.

3. In a 4-quart heavy pot, heat oil over low heat until hot. Cook red pepper flakes and garlic-parsley mixture for about 2 minutes, mixing, until garlic starts to sizzle.

4. Bring heat up to medium-high, add the squid, for about 1 minute, cook and stir occasionally until it is barely opaque.

5. Put the wine, simmering briskly and occasionally stirring, uncovered, for about 10 minutes until it reduces slightly.

6. With their juice add tomatoes, 1/2 tsp. pepper, 1 1/4 tsps. salt, and water.

7. Simmer, occasionally stirring, covered, for 30-40 minutes until squid is very tender.

8. Season with extra pepper and salt. Stir in leftover parsley.

Cioppino Seafood Stew

Fantastic for guests and perfect for day before prep.

Serves: 6

Time: 1h

Ingredients

- 3 garlic cloves, divided
- 2 tbsps. extra-virgin olive oil
- 3/4 cup finely chopped onion
- 1/2 cup packed sliced fennel
- 1/4 cup finely chopped celery
- 1 tsp. kosher salt, divided
- 1/2 tsp. freshly ground black pepper, divided
- 1/2 tsp. red-pepper flakes
- 1/2 lb. squid, cleaned, tentacles halves, bodies sliced into thick rings
- 1/2 tbsp. tomato paste
- 1 tsp. dried oregano
- 1 cup dry white wine
- 1 15-oz. canned tomatoes, crushed
- 2 bay leaves
- 1 8-oz. bottle clam juice
- 1 1/2 cups fish stock
- 4 tbsps. butter, unsalted, room temperature
- 3 tbsps. parsley, chopped, divided
- 1/2 tsp. lemon zest
- 1 baguette, sliced and toasted
- 1 lb. littleneck clams, soaked

- 1/2 lb. shrimp, peeled and deveined, tail on
- 1 lb. mussels, scrubbed and de-bearded
- 1/2 lb. white fish, skinless, flaky, cubed

Directions

1. Mince 2 garlic cloves. Heat oil in a big pot on medium heat. Add 1/4 tsp. pepper, 1/2 tsp. salt, celery, fennel, and onion.

2. Cook for 6-8 minutes, occasionally stirring, until soft. Add red pepper flakes and minced garlic. Keep cooking, constantly stirring, for another 1-2 minutes until garlic is fragrant and golden.

3. Reduce heat down to medium low. Add squid. Cook for 15-20 minutes, occasionally stirring, until squid is tender and opaque and released juices reduce a bit. Add oregano and tomato paste. Cook while stirring for 1 minute.

4. Add wine, bring heat to medium high. Cook for 5-7 minutes until cooking liquid reduces to half. Add tomatoes with their juice, stock, clam juice, and bay leaves. Boil, reduce to simmer, then cook for 30 minutes, covered. Mix in 1/4 tsp. each of pepper and salt. Taste then adjust seasonings.

5. As it cooks, mix 1/4 tsp. salt, lemon zest, 1 tbsp. parsley, and butter in a small bowl. Cut garlic clove to half. Rub cut sides on toasts. Spread flavored butter on toasts.

6. For serving time, heat pot to medium. Add clams and cook for 3 minutes, covered. Mix in mussels and shrimp. Place shrimp on stew. Simmer, covered, for about 5 minutes more until shrimp and fish are opaque and firm and shellfish opens. Throw out bay leaves. Mix in leftover 2 tbsps. parsley.

7. Immediately serve cioppino in big soup bowls. Put gremolata toasts on the side.

8. You can make base up until making the clams and keep in the fridge overnight. Reheat base and add seafood in order given above to serve.

Charred Chiles And Squid Salad

If spicy food is your thing, this recipe is for you.

Serves: 4

Time: 40 mins

Ingredients

- 1/2 Serrano, sliced thinly into rings
- 2 tbsps. fresh lime juice
- 1 tsp. fish sauce
- 3 tbsps. olive oil
- 1/4 tsp. sugar
- Kosher salt, freshly ground pepper
- 1 cup basil
- 2 cups chiles, Padrón
- 1/2 lb. squid, tentacles halved, bodies cut into rings
- 1 tbsp. plus 1 tsp. vegetable oil
- 1 tsp. pepper, Aleppo-style
- 1 cup cilantro

Directions

1. In a small bowl, whisk sugar, fish sauce, lime juice, olive oil, and serrano chile. Season vinaigrette with pepper and salt.

2. Slice 2 chiles very thinly into rings. Add into vinaigrette. Let stand for 10 minutes.

3. In a big skillet, heat 1 tbsp. vegetable oil over medium-high. Pat dry squid with paper towel. Sprinkle Aleppo-style pepper then season with pepper and salt.

4. Cook for about 1 minute, undisturbed, until the bottom side is golden brown.

5. Toss squid and keep cooking for about 1 minute longer, tossing often, until they're cooked through. Place in a medium bowl. Wipe skillet out.

6. In a skillet, heat leftover 1 tsp. vegetable oil. Cook leftover chiles for about 5 minutes, occasionally tossing, until browned in spots, blistered, and crisp-tender.

7. Place chiles in bowl with squid. Add basil, cilantro and vinaigrette with sliced chiles. Toss until combined. Season using pepper and salt.

Coconut Octopus Salad

The sweetness from the coconut in this dish greatly complements this tasty octopus salad.

Serves: 4

Time: 3 hrs. 30 mins

Ingredients

- 1 lb. octopus, cleaned, sliced into thin rings
- 1 small pepper, Serrano, minced
- 1 pepper, Fresno, red, thinly sliced
- 1/4 cup lime juice
- 3 tbsps. green onion, chopped, divided
- 2 tbsps. coconut milk
- 1 tbsp. fish sauce, or to taste
- 1 tbsp. rice wine vinegar
- 1 tsp. palm sugar
- 2 tbsps. vegetable oil
- 2/3 cup coconut flakes, unsweetened, toasted
- 1/2 cup cilantro, chopped
- 1 tsp. lime juice

Directions

1. In a big bowl, mix palm sugar, rice wine vinegar, fish sauce, coconut milk, 2 tbsps. green onion, lime juice, fresno pepper, serrano pepper, and octopus.

2. Cover plastic wrap on bowl. Keep in fridge for 2-3 hours to blend flavors.

3. Pour octopus mixture in a colander above a bowl or sink. Drain for about 5 minutes. Throw out liquid.

4. In a big skillet, heat oil on high heat until the oil smokes. Sauté octopus mixture for about 1 minute in hot oil until octopus firms and turns white.

5. Pour mixture in a big shallow serving bowl. Cool down to room temperature. Wrap then keep in fridge for about 1 hour until cold.

6. Toss accumulated juices and octopus in a bowl. Add leftover green onion, lime juice, cilantro, and coconut flakes. Mix.

30 Minute Octopus Calamari

This delicious dish can be whipped up in half an hour and is extremely tasty.

Serves: 5

Time: 30 mins

Ingredients

- 2 lbs. octopus, cleaned, cut into rings
- 1 tsp. salt
- 1 cup flour, all-purpose
- 1/2 cup vegetable oil
- 1 pinch black pepper, ground

Directions

1. Rinse then drain octopus well. Pat dry octopus using paper towels. Sprinkle salt onto octopus.

2. In a small plastic/paper bag, put flour and several octopus. Shake octopus rounds in bag until coated. Take out octopus and put more in the bag to coat.

3. In a medium-sized frying pan, heat oil on high heat. Fry calamari in oil until crispy and golden brown. Drain calamari onto paper towels. Serve while hot.

Squid Soup

This dish provides modern delicious twist on an Italian classic.

Serves: 4

Time: 35 mins

Ingredients

- 4 tbsps. olive oil, extra-virgin
- 2 lbs. white fish, firm fillet
- 1/2 lb. scallops, cleaned and halved
- 1/2 lb. shrimp, cleaned
- 1/2 lb. squid, cleaned and diced
- 3 garlic cloves, minced
- 1/4 tsp. saffron threads, crushed
- 24 clams, littleneck, scrubbed
- 24 mussels, scrubbed and debearded
- 1 cup white wine, dry
- 1 tsp. red pepper flakes, dried
- 3 Roma tomatoes, peeled, seeded, and chopped
- 1/4 cup loosely packed fresh flat-leaf parsley, coarsely chopped
- 1/4 cup loosely packed fresh basil leaves, torn
- 4 cups fish stock
- Kosher salt and freshly ground black pepper

Directions

1. Warm oil in a big pot on moderate heat. Sear fish fillets for about 4 minutes in total until both sides are brown. Add and cook garlic, squid, shrimp, and scallops in the pan, very gently stirring, for 1 minute until garlic becomes aromatic.

2. Add then boil half of basil, about half of parsley, tomatoes, pepper flakes, white wine, mussels, clams, and saffron. Reduce heat then simmer for 2 minutes to start cooking seafood.

3. Add water or fish stock. Boil again the liquids. Cover pot with a tight lid. Simmer for 4-5 minutes until mussels and clams completely opened. Throw out the ones that don't open.

4. Add leftover parsley and basil. Season with pepper and salt. Ladle soup gently in bowls. Keep as many whole fish pieces as you can.

Fried Squid with Pineapple

This sweet and crispy dish is the perfect afternoon snack.

Serves: 4

Time: 20 mins

Ingredients

- 2 tbsps. vegetable oil
- 3 cloves garlic, minced
- 1 onion, cut into wedges
- 2 lbs. squid, cleaned and cut into thick rings
- 1/2 pineapple - peeled, cored and chopped
- 4 celery stalks, cut into 2 inch pieces
- 4 tbsps. fish sauce
- 1 tsp. white sugar
- 1 tsp. black pepper, ground

Directions

1. Heat oil and garlic in a big skillet on medium-high heat. Fry until garlic becomes golden brown.

2. Add onion then stir fry for 1 minute. Add squid then cook until they become white, don't overcook.

3. Add pepper, sugar, fish sauce, celery, and pineapple. Stir fry it for 2 minutes.

Greek Squid

This stew is authentic and delicious.

Serves: 4

Time: 1 hr. 30 min

Ingredients

- 2 lbs. squid, cleaned and cut into chunks
- 2 onions, medium, chopped finely
- 2 bay leaves
- 5 cloves, whole
- 1 cinnamon stick
- 2 cups red wine, dry
- 1/3 cup olive oil
- 1/3 cup malt vinegar
- 1/4 tsp. black pepper, ground

Directions

1. In a big saucepan, put bay leaves, cloves, cinnamon stick, onions, and squid.

2. Cover then simmer for about 10 minutes on low heat.

3. As it simmers, squid will release its juices. Uncover the pan. Simmer until juices mostly evaporated. Take out bay leaves, cloves, and cinnamon stick.

4. Mix in pepper, malt vinegar, wine, and olive oil. Cover then cook for about 1 hour on low heat, occasionally stirring. Place in bowls. Serve.

Conclusion

That's all for now. Thank you for reading through the From Octopus to Squid Cookbook. I hope you enjoyed reading, cooking and tasting all

30 simple, inventive delicious octopus recipes that were set to leave your guests wanting more.

If you enjoyed what you read through, please take a few minutes to leave an honest review on the platform on which you purchased the book. Thanks again for joining me on the culinary journey. I wish you joy and good food.

Cheers!

About the Author

Born in New Germantown, Pennsylvania, Stephanie Sharp received a Masters degree from Penn State in English Literature. Driven by her passion to create culinary masterpieces, she applied and was accepted to The International Culinary School of the Art Institute where she excelled in French cuisine. She has married her cooking skills with an aptitude for business by opening her own small cooking school where she teaches students of all ages.

Stephanie's talents extend to being an author as well and she has written over 400 e-books on the art of cooking and baking that include her most popular recipes.

Sharp has been fortunate enough to raise a family near her hometown in Pennsylvania where she, her husband and children live in a beautiful rustic house on an extensive piece of land. Her other passion is taking care of the furry members of her family which include 3 cats, 2 dogs and a potbelly pig named Wilbur.

Watch for more amazing books by Stephanie Sharp coming out in the next few months.

Author's Afterthoughts

I am truly grateful to you for taking the time to read my book. I cherish all of my readers! Thanks ever so much to each of my cherished readers for investing the time to read this book!

With so many options available to you, your choice to buy my book is an honour, so my heartfelt thanks at reading it from beginning to end!

I value your feedback, so please take a moment to submit an honest and open review on Amazon so I can get valuable insight into my readers' opinions and others can benefit from your experience.

Thank you for taking the time to review!

Stephanie Sharp

For announcements about new releases, please

follow my author page on Amazon.com!

You can find that at:

https://www.amazon.com/author/stephanie-sharp

*or Scan **QR-code** below.*

Printed in Great Britain
by Amazon